Almost Missing Heaven

Terry Hurt

ISBN
978-1-959314-13-4 (Paperback)
978-1-959314-14-1 (eBook)
978-1-959314-12-7 (Hardcover)

Acknowledgment

I wish to express my gratitude to my wife, Eunice, for her having the patience with me while spending hours in preparation for this book. Then she took my original manuscript, which, for the most part, was difficult to read and understand, and typed it, making it ready for the next phase.

Also, I want to thank a great and longtime friend, Leslie Sakolnik, who proofread and made corrections and typeset the manuscript. She did a fantastic job designing the cover also!

Most importantly, I want to thank the Lord Jesus Christ who inspired me to create this book and guided me by His Holy Spirit from the beginning to the end. To God be the glory!

Preface

The contents of this book are presented to readers of all ages to help them understand where they are presently and where they can be in the future if they will accept a change in their lives, hearts, and souls with the reward of heaven eternally.

Almost Missing Heaven

This is a true testimony of a man who, one day, almost missed heaven.

Have you ever really stopped to give that statement any real serious thought? Have you thought that perhaps even you, dear reader, might be walking in that same man's shoes? As you read this account, could you, too, be on the pathway to almost missing heaven?

For one to miss out on heaven would be the most tragic and unrewarding experience one could ever find oneself in.

As you journey through this life, you can be faced with many hurtful trials and tribulations. More often than not, in most cases over a period of time, there is a healing process. However, if you happen to miss heaven and discover yourself in hell, you will be there for all eternity without any hope for a chance of release or anyone to help you escape from that dreadful place.

Think with me, won't you please, for just a moment on that word *heaven*. Heaven actually is a real place that has been around since before the beginning of time itself. With this thought, it behooves me to mention these two—time and heaven—have never existed, one without the other and have always been inseparable.

The very first verse in the Bible tells us that "in the beginning God created the heaven and the earth" (Gen. 1:1).

Let us meditate for just a moment about heaven. Did you know heaven is mentioned at least 562 times in the Bible? If it was so imperative for the Lord to mention heaven so many times, it should behoove us to pay very close attention to His directive.

Heaven is a real place where God abides. Actually, the Bible explains this heaven to be the third heaven. The first heaven is what the naked eye may observe—the atmospheric elements just above the earth. The first heaven is where we see the clouds from which we receive rain upon the earth, thunder is heard, lightening observed, and the birds fly therein.

There is an account in the Bible recorded in 2 Corinthians 12:2 and 4, where the Apostle Paul says, "I knew a man in Christ above fourteen years ago (whether in the body, I cannot tell; or whether out of the body, I cannot tell: God knoweth) such a one caught up to the third heaven... How that he was caught up into paradise, and heard unspeakable words, which it is not lawful for a man to utter."

Another recorded account in Scripture is found in Revelation 4:1 when the Apostle John was called up into heaven and was shown things that were to come to pass. The Apostle John was the one God had chosen to reveal the future events that would come upon and affect the earth and earth dwellers. So John's spirit was brought up to heaven to receive the instructions from God by His angel. He penned these things while he was exiled to the island of Patmos. John recorded these things that were revealed to him, which will literally happen based on God's time clock.

One other account is found in Acts 7:55-60, when Stephen was allowed to see into heaven just before he died as he was being stoned.

> Behold I see the heavens opened, and the Son of man standing on the right hand of God... And they stoned Stephen calling upon God and saying, Lord Jesus, receive my spirit. (vss. 56 and 59)

Since we have the account of an existing third heaven, it also means there must be a first and second heaven—the first heaven we have already mentioned, which God allows the human eye to see. Just above the first heaven is the second heaven, which would consist of the universe—all the planets, the stars with all the stellar properties and where we would more than likely find the presence of angelic beings.

The Bible explains to us that one day, the first heaven, the second heaven, and the present earth will be done away with. God will remake this all new.

As quoted before, the Bible has much to say about heaven, and we know the Bible speaks of heaven as being a beautiful place. There are many scriptures in the Bible that tell us of the beauty of heaven with all its splendor. It is no wonder that the human race has a difficult time wrapping their minds around the concept of heaven.

We all know—and the Bible affirms—the reason Jesus left heaven and came to earth was to provide the only way for us to go to heaven at the end of our journey here on earth.

Someone might ask, "Who is Jesus?" The Bible clearly explains to us He is God's only begotten Son, the only One who was acceptable by God's standard to redeem man back to God enabling man to go to heaven. The Bible tells us that without the shedding of blood, there is no remission of sin. Jesus was sent by God to be the only savior of all generations of people by shedding His blood. Having known no sin, His was the only blood acceptable to God in order to redeem fallen man back into the grace of God. Man fell away from God in the Garden of Eden, which is covered a bit later.

Just before Jesus finished His mission here on earth, He spoke to His disciples in the Book of John:

> Let not your heart be troubled: ye believe in God, believe also in me. In my Father's house are many mansions: if it were not so, I would have told you. I go to prepare a place for you. And if I go and prepare a place for you, I will come again, and receive you unto myself; that where I am, there ye may be also. And whither I go ye know, and the way ye know... Jesus said, "I am the way, the truth, and the life: no man cometh unto the Father, but by me" (John 14:1—4, 6)

Also 2 Timothy 2:5 says,

> For there is one God, and one mediator between God and men, the man Christ Jesus.

Jesus is saying very simply that no one can go to heaven, except they go through Him.

Just think, dear reader, of all the heartache and hurtful experience we may find ourselves dealing with every day— all the pain, suffering, and agony it brings on, whether it be mental or physical, as we make our journey through this life on earth.

We know that in heaven, there will be no more separation from loved ones, no more worrying about things. No more need for doctors, hospitals, lawyers, funeral homes, or bankers because no one will have any debt to pay. And the list can go on as one's mind can think of more things that will not be in heaven to bring us hardship of any kind.

I think you can truthfully say in your heart that someday heaven is where you will want to be. You can be with God because He has left that choice up to you— only you can decide where you will spend eternity.

However, there is one thing of importance to remember, we do not know at what time we will be called from our earthly lives to appear before

God. Some folks think they have a lot of time left to make a decision for Christ. On the contrary, we have absolutely no control when our lives will come to an end—as an infant or toddler, grade school student or high schooler, middle-aged person or a senior adult. Then we must appear before the Lord and give an account to Him for the way we lived our lives on the earth.

My mind takes me to a story in the Bible in the book of Luke about a man of whom the Lord spoke. He possessed land which brought forth plentifully and he had no more room to store his bountiful supply.

> And he said, This will I do: I will pull down my barns, and build greater; and there will I bestow all my fruits and my goods. And I will say to my soul, Soul, thou hast much goods laid up for many years; take thine ease, eat, drink, and be merry. But God said unto him, Thou fool, this night thy soul shall be required of thee: then whose shall those things be, which thou hast provided? (Luke 12:18-29)

The man thought he had a lot of time to live and enjoy his bounty; however, God called him to appear before Him ending his life on earth.

Just a couple of real-life experiences I learned from the writing of Oliver B. Greene, who was a great man of God and a great preacher of the Gospel, who has written many great books, and who has experienced these two testimonies. He quotes those in one of his books he titled the *Greatest Question* on page 13 and 14.

Quote from the *Greatest Question* by Oliver B. Greene, of The Gospel Hour (pp. 13-14)

> Some years ago a dear old gentleman asked me to come talk with him about his soul. He died during the course of our conversation, although he was apparently as healthy as any person I have ever seen when I arrived at his home. He asked me this question: "What did you say the other morning about being born again? What is the new birth?" After turning to John chapter three in my Bible and reading the first five verses, I paused to explain the new birth; and when I lifted my eyes from my Bible, the old gentleman was dead! The last words that man said were: "Mr. Greene, what did you say about being born again?"

On another occasion, a young man sat in one of my meetings. He was unsaved, and when I asked him to come to Jesus he said, "Preacher, when I get *ready* to be saved, I will *be* saved. You will not need to come for me, I will come forward myself." The next morning that young man suffered a severe heart attack and was unconscious until the next day. When he regained consciousness, his pastor and I instructed him from the Word of God in the plan of salvation, and he prayed an unforgettable prayer: "God, be merciful to me a sinner. Forgive me my sins, come into my heart and save me! Lord, I am sorry I put it off until You seemingly struck me down... but Lord, have mercy on me and save me!" He had regained consciousness just long enough to trust Jesus, then dropped into a coma and died.

These two experiences give strength to what I am trying to convey to you dear reader. There is an old saying that goes something like this, "Don't put off to do tomorrow what you can do today." I liken this to salvation; the Bible says today is the accepted day of salvation not tomorrow since we have no guarantee of our tomorrow. In James 4:14, it says, "Whereas ye know not what shall be on the morrow." If you understand in your heart the Holy Spirit is calling to you, respond to Him now and don't forfeit heaven because you want to wait for a more convenient time, which might never come before your last breath of life here on earth. Eternity then will belong to you in heaven or hell. I would advise you to give this some serious meditation.

Getting back to our story, we meet a man who tells of his father and mother. His father was raised in Council, Virginia, while his mother was raised in Cleveland, Virginia. His father's name was William, and his mother's name was Ruth, who was his biological mother.

When the man of our story was aged between two and three, God deemed it necessary to call his biological mother home to heaven. I believe she was thirty-one when God called her home to heaven. So he never experienced the pleasure of knowing his biological mother or of growing up with her. But God gave him a Christian stepmother who raised him. So you see, dear reader friend, we have nothing to do with the time we are called to make our presence before God, and there is no guarantee of your life's span here on earth. You have no assurance of living to a certain age. Death may come at any age.

If you happen to a be a young person who is reading this account and still have both of your parents, a bit of advice, love them with all your heart and be obedient to them. The Bible explicitly states in the Old Testament,

> Honor thy father and thy mother: that thy days may be long upon the land which the Lord thy God giveth thee. (Exod. 20:12)

It's also in the New Testament.

> Children, obey your parents in the Lord: for this is right. Honor thy father and mother; which is the first commandment with promise; That it may be well with thee, and thou mayest live long on the earth. (Eph. 6:1-3)

So there you have it from God Himself. He who cannot lie, promises to allow longevity of life on the earth for those who will pay honor to their father and mother.

Even so, my friend, someday you and I will come to that point in time when we will look into the face of death and our destiny will be decided. Where will we spend eternity forever? You will either spend eternity in one of two places *heaven or hell.*

God lets you choose your own destiny; He does not make that choice for you. If you follow God's plan, you will be in heaven when you die. If you follow the devil's plan, you will be in hell when you die.

Sometimes while driving down the highway, you may occasionally see a sign which states, "Prepare to Meet Thy God," and that is just exactly what we have to do while God has given us the time to do so. If we procrastinate, time may expire making it eternally too late.

Other signs we can observe while driving on the road will show our destination routes and also advisory signs that keep us from danger.

God also has given us His Word to follow and warning signs to keep us from going astray. If we follow God's signs, we will arrive safely home in heaven. If you ignore God's plan, you will arrive in hell for eternity being then too late to turn around.

This man's father (William) and mother (Ruth) were married and lived in Virginia. When the pressure of the falling economy was upon the area, he moved his family to Dayton, Ohio. He was hired by Delco

Products, a division of General Motors Company, where he worked as a tool and die maker for forty-seven years.

William and Ruth were blessed with four children. The man of our story, who went by the name of Butch, had a brother whose name was William Eugene after his father, though everyone called him Gene; and two older sisters, Patricia JoAnn, who just went by JoAnn, and Carolyn, who was nicknamed Punkin.

While living in Dayton, Ruth took very ill with cancer and, after a long and painful struggle, lost her life here on earth. Back in those days, they did not possess the advanced technology to combat this disease. However, being as she was a godly woman, God welcomed her into the portals of heaven where she is today waiting for the rest of her family to join her.

William, who loved Ruth very much, became very distraught with God because he could not understand why God would take his loving wife, leaving him with four very young children to raise.

Time after time, people all across the globe find themselves in this same situation. Their lives being interrupted by some catastrophic, life-changing event, causing shipwreck of their lives. This causes much heartache and painful conditions with sorrows and sometimes resentment.

Most of the time, they find themselves blaming God for their misfortune. Most of the time, the fault is not with God Himself, but rather, from the choices and decisions that are made while living their lives on earth.

This is not something new, but it has been happening from the beginning of mankind whom God placed on the earth, whom He created in His own image to have fellowship with Him. Just a reminder, God has allowed mankind to have free will with his choices and decisions. God will not force one to follow Him or to love Him.

As you may recall, the Bible says the Lord God planted a garden in Eden and placed His first created couple, Adam and Eve, in this beautiful garden. God instructed them to care for the beautiful garden but to stay away from a certain forbidden tree that if they were to eat the fruit thereof, they would surely die. But the serpent tricked them through Eve to eat of the forbidden tree, and because they disobeyed God's instruction, God was very displeased with them.

As punishment, He chased them from the beautiful garden of plenty and cursed the ground. As a result, Adam had to labor hard by the sweat of his brow to make their living. Sin was born into the heart and lives of our first parents and has been passed down throughout the eons of time. It is still present with us today, and we are still reaping from the wrong choices in life.

Since the fall of Adam and Eve, every person born is naturally born into sin, which must be personally dealt with. The Bible tells us that our lives are short and full of troubles. James 4:14 says,

> Whereas ye know not what shall be on the morrow. For what is your life? It is even a vapor, that appeareth for a little time, and then vanisheth away.

Also, in the Book of Romans it says,

> For all have sinned, and come short of the glory of God. (Rom. 3:23)

Meaning that because we possess sin in our lives, we fall short of being good enough of the expectation or approval of God for Him to accept us into heaven as we are presently.

Something has to take place in our lives to rectify our sin and enable us to meet God's standard and approval to be accepted into heaven. However, the Bible makes it clear that not all calamities of life are sin originated. For example, in the Gospel of John, chapter 9, speaks of a man who was born blind from his birth and the disciples of Jesus asked Him,

> "Who did sin, this man, or his parents, that he was born blind?" Jesus answered, "Neither hath this man sinned, nor his parents: but that the works of God should be made manifest in him." (vss. 2-3)

Meaning that God allowed this blindness to come upon this man that He might show the world at the time when Jesus walked among men the healing power God gave to His Son, Jesus. He was the only one who could perform this miracle that allowed many to believe that Jesus is all who He claims to be.

There are many other miracles recorded in the Bible— too many to mention here—that directed attention to the glory of God through Christ Jesus. The finite mind of man is prone to have thoughts that most sicknesses and suffering are direct results of sin. Contrary to this, sometimes things happen for the only reason of bringing wandering hearts to Him (Jesus) for salvation and to glorify God.

However, one example of sickness due to one's sin can be found recorded in the Bible in the Book of John, chapter 5. Jesus had gone up to Jerusalem and entered a sheep market where there was a pool of water, which contained five porches that housed a multitude of impotent folk— some who were blind, halt, or had withered limbs and were waiting for the moving of the water.

An angel went down at a certain season into the pool and troubled the waters, and the first person to step into the water afterward was made whole of whatever disease he had. One particular man had an infirmity for thirty-eight years and was not able to move to the water on his own accord.

When Jesus asked him if he would like to be made whole, he said to Jesus that when the water was troubled, no man was able to help him into the pool, and someone would always get there before he could get into the water. Then Jesus performed another miracle and healed this man and told him to rise, take up his bed, and walk. Immediately, the man was healed and did as Jesus said.

The Bible does not explain to us what the sin was that caused this man to be in the condition he was in. However, Jesus instructed him to sin no more lest a worse thing come upon him.

So once again, dear reader, I confirm that a lot of our sicknesses may result from our lifestyles, resulting from sin because of the choices we make while traveling through this life.

I do believe that one can actually sin his or her life away, which could lead to an early or premature death. As recorded in 1 John 5:16,

> If any man see his brother sin a sin which is not unto death, he shall ask, and he shall give him life for them that sin not unto death. There is a sin unto death: I do not say that he shall pray for it.

Now this man's father, William, found himself struggling to meet the criteria of working a full-time job and meeting the demands of a household. Since it was not working as good as it should, he sent out a plea through the local newspaper for a helping hand.

After several helpers came and went, things just weren't working as well as he had hoped it would. The older brother and two sisters were running the streets of Dayton, sometimes footloose and fancy-free, doing at will all their little minds could think of. This brought much heartache to the father because he thought he should have more control of the children. It is always best to have both a father and mother raising and training the children in their home.

Train up a child in the way he should go: and when he is old, he will not depart from it. (Prov. 22:6)

He that spareth his rod hateth his son: but he that loveth him chasteneth him betimes. (Prov. 13:24)

Foolishness is bound in the heart of a child, but the rod of correction shall drive it far from him. (Prov. 22:15)

Withhold not correction from the child: for if thou beatest him with the rod, he shall not die. Thou shall beat him with the rod, and shalt deliver his soul from hell. (Prov. 23:13,14)

So, dear reader, if you have small children, raising them up and training them in a biblical way will, one day, bring much comfort for you and your children. I cannot help but wonder that raising children the biblical way might make our jails and prisons less occupied and, in some cases, prevent premature death. So the choice to make is to train your children the way God has instructed and direct them toward heaven or ignore God's way and let Satan have them.

One day, a lady by the name of Thelma Wright came on the scene. She seemed to have more success than the previous helpers, even as this man of the story and his siblings continued to be little city terrors moving about the city streets, devising all kinds of mischief and carrying the plans out to do damage.

His father was afraid he might have to separate his older brother, Gene, from the other siblings and place him into some sort of boys' home to help bring him back to a normal way of life. This saddened his other siblings very much. They did not want to be separated, and neither did his father have a desire to separate the family.

It behooved this man's father to marry this woman, making her a permanent part of the family and becoming a stepmother to him and his siblings. The man of the story was approximately three years of age when this all took place. This lady became the only mother he ever really knew.

Earlier, we spoke of heaven being a beautiful place that brings my attention to the story of the man we are writing about. His stepmother once told him that, at one point in her life, she came face-to-face with death. However, God spared her life, so she told him the story of when she almost died. Just before that experience, she said she saw one of the most beautiful sights she had ever seen in her entire life. She said God allowed her to see a glimpse of heaven. She said, "I never want to go that far again and not go on."

As we continue to unfold this story, his stepmother has made that journey, and today, she has crossed over into that beautiful place of heaven, where we all desire to be someday. This man's Christian stepmother was the lady who raised him from a small child.

I am almost positive that you, as well, might know of a loved one or someone who has had a similar experience and now is in heaven, happily rejoicing with all heaven's splendor and beauty around them. They are there with previous loved ones gone on before them and waiting for your arrival.

After a season of time, his father thought it best to relocate his family from the city life in Dayton to an eighty- two-acre farm in Greenville, approximately thirty-five miles northwest of Dayton.

Moving a city family to a farm opened up a whole new experience for the siblings. There was plenty to learn and a whole lot of work. One of the first things the move accomplished was to get the children off the streets, which was causing a lot of heartache for him.

Now the father knew where his children were—on the farm. Soon after the move, the man of the story and his siblings found themselves engaged in feeding chickens, hogs, and sheep; milking cows the old-fashioned way—bucket between the knees, perched on a stool, hand pulling the milk from the cows.

There were fields to plow and plant and harvest after first pulling tons of rock off the field. And of course, there were long runs of fence to build. Along with all this, somehow schoolwork had to be fitted in the mix. This solved the problem of playing in the streets of the city, which gave a lot of relief for the father.

They had to get up before the rooster crowed, and in the wintertime, if it had snowed, they would find themselves trudging through snowbanks up to their knees in order to get to the barn. Then they had to milk the cows and take care of all the animals' feeding, which would oftentimes lead to going to school smelling like the farm! Then once they were home after school, they began the process all over again.

The old farmhouse had no air conditioning for the summer and in the winter heat was from an old, potbelly wood and coal stove which was fed mostly by coal. On cold winter nights when the strong, cold, snowy wind blew, you woke up in the morning to see snow had blown through the cracks in the window frames and was laying on the cold bare floors.

They would jump out of bed, grab their cold clothes and run down the stairs to dress by the warm potbelly stove only to find out that the stove had burned out through the night! It was freezing in the house! Not only that, but the cold winter night froze all the water and you couldn't even wash.

You have undoubtedly heard someone make mention of "the good ole days." I believe, dear reader, that if you had an opportunity to speak to the man of this story and his siblings, they might have a little difference of opinion.

There was a room in the old farmhouse where an old upright piano sat with a picture of his biological mother on top. As a very young boy, he would find himself in that room, many times standing in front of that piano, just staring up at her picture. He was trying to figure out and remember in his little mind what his mother was like because he was so young when she passed away.

The family would sometimes attend this little country church, but as he reached the age of approximately twelve or thirteen, he decided within himself he was no longer going to go to church. And he didn't. Why he was allowed to make this decision and was not made to attend church with his family is still unknown.

You may sometimes think at the time of your decision, you are the one making it; but if the influence of the devil can keep you from going to God's house of prayer, he's going to do what he can to keep you away. This allows him to influence you in the way he wants you to go to follow him instead of God. He will eventually drag you into hell with him, into the lake of fire where he (the devil) will finally be placed by God Himself one day soon.

And this is exactly what happened to the man of our story once he was allowed to make the decision not to go to church. The devil led him astray from God, farther and farther until the devil had him in the clutches of his hands. He guided him into all the deceptions of sin to the point he hardly ever gave God a thought anymore.

The devil had this man traveling on the course the Bible explains to be the wide gate in Matthew 7:13-14.

> Enter ye in at the strait gate: for wide is the gate, and broad is the way, that leadeth to destruction, and many there be which go in thereat: Because strait is the gate and narrow is the way, which leadeth unto life, and few there be that find it.

In a nutshell, what this means is that the devil had this man traveling on the broad way where there are many people the devil has already tricked or deceived in following him into that hellfire. Dear reader, if you happen to be one of those misfortunate, falsely guided ones on that road, it would be advantageous for you to turn around and get on the narrow, straight road leading to heaven. If you die traveling the broad road to hell, you will be bound there for an eternity, never having another chance to change your mind once you have taken your last breath of life here on earth. Your decision will have already been permanently fixed. You will spend eternity in hell, never ever being able to escape the torments prepared for those who go to hell.

In the beginning of our story, we mentioned the Bible having approximately 562 verses on heaven, now might be a good time to mention the opposite of heaven—hell. We can view heaven as being a positive and hell as being a negative. All things mentioned about heaven are good, and all things mentioned about hell are bad.

If you conducted a poll and asked any number of people whether they would desire to receive something good or bad, I almost guarantee 100 percent of the responders would want the good thing.

Hell is a real place just like heaven, and just like heaven, if one finds himself in hell, he will have all his known senses. He will be able to see, smell, feel, taste, hear, and understand and be able to reason. There is a very well-known story in the Bible that proves this in Luke 16:19-31.

There was a certain rich man, which was clothed in purple and fine linen, and fared sumptuously every day: And there was a certain beggar named Lazarus, which was laid at his gate, full of sores, And desiring to be fed with the crumbs which fell from the rich man's table: moreover the dogs came and licked his sores. And it came to pass, that the beggar died, and was carried by the angels into Abraham's bosom: the rich man also died, and was buried; And in hell he lift up his eyes, being in torments, and seeth Abraham afar off, and Lazarus in his bosom. And he cried and said, Father Abraham, have mercy on me, and send Lazarus, that he may dip the tip of his finger in water, and cool my tongue; for I am tormented in this flame. But Abraham said, Son, remember that thou in thy lifetime receivedst thy good things, and likewise Lazarus evil things: but now he is comforted, and thou art tormented. And beside all this, between us and you there is a great gulf fixed: so that they which would pass from hence to you cannot; neither can they pass to us, that would come from thence. Then he said, I pray thee therefore, father, that thou wouldest send him to my father's house: For I have five brethren; that he may testify unto them, lest they also come into this place of torment. Abraham saith unto him, They have Moses and the prophets; let them hear them. And he said, Nay, Father Abraham: but if one went unto them from the dead, they will repent. And he said unto him, If they hear not Moses and the prophets, neither will they be persuaded, though one rose from the dead.

The statement "Abraham's bosom," figuratively speaking, means to occupy the seat next or closest to Abraham. Abraham was in the paradise of God.

Also, the Scripture speaks of the rich man being in hell. That does not signify that all rich people go to hell. That person just happened to be a very wealthy person. However, Jesus does tell His disciples in Mark 10:23 and 24,

> How hardly shall they that have riches enter into the kingdom of God! And the disciples were astonished at his words. But Jesus answereth again, and saith unto them, Children, how hard is it for them that trust in riches to enter into the kingdom of God!

There are some who have become very wealthy with earthly possessions, which sometimes make it harder for them to trust in Christ. They have all they want in this life, giving little thought to life after death.

Hell will not be the fun place that some people make jokes about by saying, "I am going to hell to party with my friends." People need to be awakened out of their coma because when they arrive in hell it will be a totally different experience from what they think or believe—the joke will be on them.

The choice you make in this life for the life after will be unchanging and permanent for all eternity. The only two choices you have is heaven and all its bliss or hell and all its torments.

Just a few more of the many times the Bible speaks about Hell:

Hell and destruction are never full. (Prov. 27:20)

To go into hell, into the fire that never shall be quenched: Where their worm dieth not, and the fire is not quenched. (Mark 9:43-44)

And the devil that deceived them was cast into the lake of fire and brimstone, where the beast and the false prophet are, and shall be tormented day and night for ever and ever. (Rev. 20:10)

I would like you to think about something for one moment. When you get hurt or contract a disease that inflicts great pain in your body, sometimes unbearable pain, you can get medical help to relieve the pain. However, if you end up in hell with all its torment, pain, and suffering, you will not be able to get any relief. For how long? Forever and forever.

Hell is not a place for which you will want to forfeit heaven. You cannot play around with your life here continuously and avoid salvation to the point where it becomes too late for you to accept Christ. If you die without making a decision for Christ and find yourself in hell, you will never have an opportunity to get out. You will be there for an eternity. Eternity is forever and ever, and for as long as you can say the word *forever.*

Some people believe that when they die with their sins unforgiven, they will be placed somewhere between the earth and heaven, where they will have their sins redeemed, allowing them to go on into heaven. The Bible teaches us that to be absent from the body is to be present with the Lord, if one has been born again. Even the apostle Paul says,

> Therefore we are always confident, knowing that, whilst we are at home in the body, we are absent from the Lord... We are confident, I say, and willing rather to be absent from the body, and to be present with the Lord. (2 Cor. 5:6-8)

The very moment you close your eyes in death in this life, you will open your eyes in eternity—either heaven or hell from the choice the Lord has allowed you to make.

In the story you just read about the rich man and Lazarus, it says they went immediately to their respective eternal abodes. There was no waiting time between earth and their final destination. Lazarus was immediately in the paradise of God and the rich man went immediately to hell.

God does not make the choice of heaven or hell for us. That choice is left to us to make. The Bible says in 2 Peter 3:9 that the "Lord is not slack concerning his promise, as some men count slackness but is long-suffering; to us-ward, not willing that any should perish, but that all should come to repentance." Which means the Lord shows an abundance of patience toward us throughout our lives, calling to us by His Holy Spirit, waiting for us to open the door of our hearts to let Him in. When you do, He will save you and add your name to the Lamb's Book of Life.

He has made the plan—a way to heaven—simple and free and has left us with that freedom of choice. I promise you one thing upon the Word of God, that when you take your last fleeting breath of life here on this earth, your decision will be final.

We return back to the man of our story. After his siblings moved away, it left most of the farm work to him. After a period of time, his father decided to sell the farm and relocate to a house in town, so he did. He had an auction to sell the farm and all the farm equipment, and soon, they were relocated to a house in town.

One day, this man came home from work and his mother said, "You have a letter here from the government." Not understanding why the government would send him a letter, he very inquisitively opened it only to find he had been inducted into the Armed Forces of the United States of America.

Taking the letter to the recruiting office, he enlisted into the Air Force and soon found himself boarding a bus headed to Lackland Air Force Base Training Center to begin his four-year commitment to serve in the Air Force of this great country we live in. After his six weeks of basic training, he was assigned to Travis Air Force Base in California to begin his first duty assignment.

Being based in California, he was placed in a squadron, where he met a young man named Lefaine Deaver, who became his best friend during their military time together. In all the passing years, they have managed to remain best friends. The Bible speaks about a friend that sticks closer than a brother, and he is that type of a friend.

Another friend whom he knew as a child—they grew up together, went through school together, and became the best of friends and remained such through all the years—Steve Stebbins, who still lives in Greenville, Ohio, to this day.

When the man of our story was enlisted into the Air Force, he had just purchased a brand-new 1965 Chevy Chevelle. When he was sent overseas to Germany for three years, this friend, Steve Stebbins, purchased the car from him. To this day, he still has that car. Steve Stebbins is another friend that sticks closer than a brother.

If a person has friends like these, he is a blessed person.

During the first nine months in California, he was sent TDY to the beautiful country of Guam. (Guam is an island located in the north Pacific Ocean, just north of the Pacific Island.) Upon returning back to Travis Air Force base, he heard tell from his roommate about a new, pretty WAF that had moved into the squadron and was working as the new secretary in the administration office (WAF [Women in the Air Force] After World war II, women were allowed to serve in the Air Force.) her name was Eunice Buckner. He immediately went to the office to make his acquaintance with this young lady, and after much deliberation, she finally agreed to have a date with him.

During the course of the next six months, as they were getting to know each other, he had put in a request for a tour of duty overseas because he knew he probably would not be able to afford to travel to other countries once he was released from the military back into civilian life.

Soon, he was blessed with orders to go to Europe being based at Rhine Mein Air Force Base, Germany. However, before leaving Travis Air Force Base, he said to the WAF he had met during this time, "I am going my way. You go your way, and we will see what comes of our relationship when I return." Little did he know that during the three years he was in Germany, she would write to him daily, binding their relationship.

Before leaving Travis Air Force Base, his commanding sergeant, who assisted him in getting his orders to Germany in Europe, said to him, "During your tour in Germany, you will need to keep a sharp eye out for trouble. You won't have to look for trouble. It will find you." After being in Germany for a season of time, he soon found out that the sergeant knew what he was talking about.

Through the course of the three years in Germany, he was confronted with several trying and testing situations that brought him to the mind-set that a change of life was needed. Then one day, what happened to this man was the beginning of what brought a change in his life forever. The Holy Spirit, directed by the Lord, began looking and calling for him.

That reminds me of the story of Adam and Eve. Remember how God placed them in the Garden He created and gave them instructions. They disobeyed God, and sin was born into the human race. After Adam and Eve sinned, they hid themselves from the presence of God because of the guilt of sin. God came looking and calling for them.

Even today, one cannot hide from God because He knows you by name, where you are at all times, and what you are doing. There is an old saying, "You can run, but you can't hide." The Bible says,

> For the ways of man are before the eyes of the Lord, and he pondereth all his goings. (Prov. 5:21).

With approximately six months left of his tour of duty in Germany, he decided to purchase a new car and bring it back to the states with him. Finding his way to the auto dealership, he found a car that satisfied his interest. After deciding on the Opal Rally, he placed the order and purchased it. When he was notified it was in and ready for pick up, he went to the dealership, consummated the deal, and drove it back to the air base. He was waiting until the right time to ship the car home stateside.

Meanwhile, after a season of time, he and one of his airmen friends had driven the car to a few local German establishments before going in to work. They were working a night shift from 12:00 p.m. till morning, and there was some time in the evening for a little fun before reporting to work.

As the evening raced on, and before they had realized it, there had been one too many alcoholic drinks, which were beginning to play tricks with the mind. They decided to leave their fun place because time was closing in for them to report for duty. While driving back to the base, they were following a German high-bed truck that seemed to be slowing them down.

While passing this truck, he got a little too close to the high bed on the truck and sideswiped the truck, causing a can-opener-like cut down the side of his new car. This frustrated him to no end because it was his brand-new car that meant so much to him. After all the excitement of the wreck, they were late to their job, and the night shift sergeant-in-charge was not a happy camper with them showing up for duty late and smelling of liquor. This man and the night shift sergeant engaged in a verbal attack with each other. The sergeant could have put him in jail or the stockade, but the sergeant had mercy on this man and did not ask much of him throughout the night because of his impairment.

In like manner, God shows much mercy toward us as He patiently waits for us to accept Jesus Christ as our Saviour and Lord. He is willing to forgive us our sins when we call upon Him. If you stop and really think a moment how each one of us has mistreated God in our lives, at any moment, He could say, "I am no longer going to deal with you" and snuff out your life.

However, the Bible says in Numbers 14:18,

> The Lord is longsuffering, and of great mercy, forgiving iniquity and transgression, and by no means clearing the guilty.

The Second Epistle of Peter 3:9 says,

> The Lord... is longsuffering to us-ward, not willing that any should perish, but that all should come to repentance.

Upon being relieved from his night shift, he went back to the barracks and went to bed. When he awoke, he was greeted by this small, inner voice, which said to him, "Don't do this again or next time it will be worse." Taking him by surprise, he began to ponder on what just happened. Where did this voice come from and what was the meaning of it? For days and weeks, this experience never left him, but after a period of time, it faded. However, it never completely left his mind. The man had taken the car to a shop to get it repaired and painted so it looked like new again.

Then one day, a new man wandered into the squadron on his shift. Being new to the squadron, he thought he would show him the town. So after visiting a few establishments and, after a few drinks dulling his memory of the inner voice, he met up with an army man while at one of the establishments. They began to boast with each other who had the fastest car, and that just had to be proven. Leaving the local establishment and while impaired from the alcohol flowing through his veins, he and his friend entered his car readying themselves for the race. Now, this man never would buckle his seatbelt, but for some reason, he buckled his and told his rider to do the same. Entering the highway, the two cars lined up and the race began.

The man remembered passing his opponent, the army guy, running about ninety miles per hour, when his passenger said to him as they were fast approaching the turnoff to go into another town. "Are you not going to take this turn?" Immediately, the man hit his brakes hard and turned the steering wheel, which put the car into a left-nose slide.

Unable to bring the car back in control, it slammed into a high concrete curb in the middle of the road. The car went airborne, coming to rest, just before going through the guardrail and down over a steep embankment.

Opening the door to get out, he noticed the road was closer to the bottom of the car than before. After investigating the situation, he found the wheels had been driven up into the body of the car from the impact. He had the car towed back to the air base and again got it ready for the second time to go to the repair shop.

Being saddened and upset with what had happened, he went to bed for the night. Waking up the following morning, he remembered what was said to him by the small, inner voice the first time. "Don't do this again, or the next time it will be worse." And it was worse. The car was so badly damaged, it spent three months in the repair shop.

The body damage was so extensive, he had to have the whole car repainted. Since yellow was his favorite color, he asked the Germans to repaint the car real bright yellow. And so it was. The small, inner voice that said to him the first time "Don't do it again or it will be worse" was right.

Once again, he pondered in his heart though not understanding the meaning of the second visitation of this inner voice speaking to him. But he did understand that what he had heard in the past came to be a truth and a reality in his life. For many days he meditated on this second warning of this small, inner voice not being able to completely understand the why or the reasoning.

After a season of time passed by, the second warning began to fade from his mind—but not completely forgotten. Then one day, another misfortunate experience visited him. As he was nearing the end of his duty in Germany to return to the United States to be discharged from the Air Force, being warned twice before—each time being worse than the time before— his life was impacted enough that he decided to take it upon himself to change his direction in life. He would introduce a new lifestyle for his life attempting to avoid future catastrophes.

Taking all this to heart, he said to himself, *I am going to change my lifestyle and do what is right.* The day soon came for him to board the airplane back to the States. Before boarding, he had only a partial pack of cigarettes left, and one of the things he had sworn off was smoking, along with drinking and other things that would cause a man heartache and drag him down.

As mentioned earlier, the devil had him just where he wanted him to be, setting him up to steal his soul.

Putting all this together, he finally began to understand that perhaps God was trying to get his attention.

After returning to the States, he was discharged from the Air Force. Then he went to the shipyard and picked up the car he shipped back from Germany. After receiving the car, he did a complete check to make sure it was road worthy. Leaving New Jersey, he drove back to his home in Greenville, Ohio.

This man's father was a devout Mason, and his older brother was also a Mason. His father wanted him to become a Mason. It would make his father a proud man to have both of his sons in the Masons with him. With this man now understanding that God was trying to get his attention, he thought it might be a good thing to join the Masons. He had learned that the Masons were founded in Christianity, so he thought through the Masons he might find God. So he did begin the process to become a Mason.

Joining the Masons, he began working hard and studying laboriously to become accepted as one of the brothers. He soon graduated to the thirty-second degree with high honors. He was gifted with a special ring, which he wore on his finger to identify himself as a brother. He was also presented with a masonic Bible.

He began asking himself, *Where do I start reading this Bible?* In searching for God, not knowing any difference, he began reading at the first chapter of the Bible in the book of Genesis. He would find himself in his bedroom at nights reading Genesis, trying to understand what he was reading. He would attend the meetings the Masonic Lodge would conduct, still searching for God.

Remember that WAF he met at Travis Air Force Base in California? She wrote him daily while he was in Germany for three years. He drove to Grand Ridge, Illinois, where she was from and brought her back to his hometown where she lived with his stepsister while they continued to build their relationship. During this time, he continued to stay at home with his parents.

One evening, when he did not have a date with her, he went to town by himself and met up with one of his longtime friends. They rode around in his friend's car, reacquainting themselves. It was not long after being in his friend's car that his friend lit up a cigarette. He had sworn off smoking and was being faithful not to smoke, but the smoke filled his nostrils and re-excited his desire to smoke again. He finally asked his friend for a cigarette, and it started all over again.

One other time, at night, while he was walking along in the cool of the evening, he stopped for a moment and gazed at the stars. At this moment, an untamed fear came over him, and he said to himself, *God is going to kill me.*

After a short season of time, he became engaged to this lady, and she continued to live with his stepsister until the time he felt the need to bring her into his life as his wife. They went back to the little town of Grand Ridge, Illinois, where she was from and were married in a little Methodist church. Afterward, they returned back to the little house they had purchased in Greenville, Ohio, and began to set up housekeeping. And a new chapter began in his life.

Then a day came when his mother asked him to come and go to church with her on a Sunday. Reasoning within himself that it would not hurt anything to accommodate his mother's wishes since he was trying to figure out and find out about God, he agreed to accompany her. He had not been to church for many years, except when he got married.

When the next Sunday arrived, he and his new bride found the church house where his mother was a member, went inside, and sat down, waiting for the service to begin. After all the different reports and the singing and the passing of the plates, the preacher began his sermon for the morning.

As this man listened very intently to the message, it happened again. This small, inner voice that had spoken to him before, spoke to him once again during the message. At the close of the message, the congregation sang a song of invitation. The preacher voiced a plea to the congregation that if anyone felt he was being called of the Lord to come forward to the front where the preacher was for instruction, or help with a decision for salvation, to do so at that time.

Being tugged in his heart from this small, inner voice very strongly, he felt he needed to do this and answer the call. Then he noticed this other stronghold within him, holding him back from doing what his heart was telling him to do. So he stood there with his hands clutched so tight to the back of the pew in front of him his knuckles turned white. He felt embarrassed to leave his pew and walk down that aisle in front of all those people he did not know. After the invitation was over, he felt some relief it was over and that he could go home.

But not quite yet. After the preacher had the ending prayer, people began to leave their seats. But this older, gray-haired man, who was a deacon of the church, found his way in front of this man. They were about the same size in height, so he looked this man square in his eyes and asked him, "Do you know Jesus Christ?"

This man being much astonished by his question and being in a church, reasoned with himself, *I don't want to tell a lie in church.* So he responded, "Well, no, I guess that is why I am here that I might learn." He left the church house with the question the man asked, "Do you know Jesus Christ?" leaving an impression on his finite mind, not understanding the meaning.

This man would find himself being drawn back to that little church from time to time, listening to the preacher's sermons. He would continually experience the small voice, attempting to get him to leave his seat during the altar call and come forward to talk with the preacher. Anytime he got enough courage to go forward, this other stronghold within would hold him back.

During this man's daily activities this little inner voice would come to him and try to get this man to go and talk to the man from the church who asked him that question, "Do you know Jesus Christ?" For some reason, that man of our story had built up enough confidence in the man from the church that he felt comfortable to talk with him. However, every time this man built up courage enough to go talk with him, that stronghold would keep him from going.

Then one day, he rode his motorcycle to the store to get some more cigars since he had started smoking again. He thought smoking cigars would help him retire from smoking cigarettes. Upon returning home and entering through the backdoor of the house, what did he see as he looked down the stairway into the basement? The man and his wife from the church.

It really startled him to think that the man was in his house. Coming up the basement stairs, the man from church greeted him with these words, "We just came over to see your new house." All of a sudden, he did not feel at ease with the man and his wife from church. Thinking within himself, *They will leave in a little bit,* but then the deacon asked for a glass of water.

Then he asked if it was all right to go into the living room, have a seat, and visit a little. This caused this man of our story to become more uncomfortable, and he waited until everyone else was seated and seated himself as far from the man as possible. It was not far enough to suit him since the little living room was only about twelve feet by twelve feet.

After a little bit of small talk and general conversation, the man began to speak on things from the Bible and of the Lord Jesus Christ. As this man of our story listened very intently to him, the small inner voice once again began to speak attempting to persuade him of his need of Jesus Christ and salvation.

As the man continued to speak to this man, he found himself being pulled very strongly between the two forces from within. The clock kept ticking, and soon, it was into the late evening. During this time of great anguish, he could feel the intense beating of his heart, and he began to break out into a sweat with much nervousness and anxiety.

As the man kept talking to him about the Lord and the Bible, he realized the Lord wanted to bring salvation to his soul and place him on the road to heaven. That other stronghold within was the devil, trying to persuade him not to go the way of the Lord because he, the devil, did not want to lose another soul. After three hours had elapsed, the man from the church figured he had exhausted all his means of persuasion, and since it was about ten o'clock in the evening, he figured it was time to go home.

The man said, "Well, I guess it is time for us to go home." Everyone stood up and was ready to bid him and his wife a goodnight. Then the man from the church said something else, realizing the Lord was really trying to get this man to open his heart and invite the Lord into his heart to make His abode with him, bring salvation to his soul, and keep his soul from going to hell one day at the end of his life here on earth.

Once again, everyone sat back down, and the man once again poured out his heart to him, hoping to persuade him to turn to the Lord before it became too late in his life.

As the man continued to talk, this man's heart began to beat stronger and harder, so heavy and loud, he could hear his heart pounding in his chest, thinking within himself that if he could hear his heart pounding that loud, everyone else in the room could surely hear his heart as well. The hard beating of the heart and the heavy perspiration caused his body to be wet. The agonizing going on within himself and his soul was nothing else but the deep conviction from all his sins, which made him feel like he was the worst person who ever walked on the face of this earth.

Being very troubled in spirit, he mounted up enough courage to say to the man from church, "If your wife and my wife will leave this house, I will talk to you." So gracefully, they removed themselves from the presence of the house, leaving the men by themselves.

This man began to talk to the man from the church telling him how burdened he was with his past and present life, how sorrowful in his heart he was, and that he really felt he was the worst person who ever walked on the face of the earth. Then he told him how he had tried to get rid of all his problems in life on his own by drinking alcohol, getting drunk, and trying to reason with himself on how to reform his life, even trying hypnosis. The only thing left to him was to end his life here on earth.

Little did this man know at that time that a man can never hope to make himself right before God or to ever do anything within himself to be accepted of God. You see in the Bible, in Isaiah 64:6, it says,

> But we are all as an unclean thing, and
> all our righteousnesses are as filthy rags.

Ephesians 2:8-9 it says,

> For by grace are ye saved through faith; and that not of yourselves: it is the gift of God: Not of works, lest any man should boast.

In other words, a person cannot do anything to earn or work his or her way to heaven by any means.

The man being deeply concerned for this man's soul, said this to him, "Just give Christ a chance in your life."

Then the man of our story said to the him, "I cannot be saved." Because within his heart, he felt he had done so much against the Lord he was not able to be saved, that the Lord would not want him.

The devil will try to do anything within his power to deceive a person, steering them away from the salvation of the Lord.

He said to the church man "Even if I was saved, it won't last a week, a month or two, and eventually, I will be right back where I started." He did not understand that he could do nothing to keep himself saved. But when a person gives his heart to the Lord, the Lord Himself keeps that person saved. Not just for a short while, but for an eternity.

Once a person puts their trust in Christ, the devil has lost the battle over that soul and can never reclaim that soul again. That soul becomes eternally secure in Christ and is heaven-bound.

Ephesians 1:13-14 says,

> In whom ye also trusted, after that ye heard the word of truth, the gospel of your salvation: in whom also after that ye believed, ye were sealed with that holy Spirit of promise. Which is the earnest of our inheritance until the redemption of the purchased possession unto the praise of his glory.

What this is saying, dear reader, is when you trust Jesus Christ as your Saviour, Jesus Christ puts His seal upon your soul and preserves you all throughout your life until He calls you to your home in heaven. He does this with His promise. Since the Bible says God does not lie, you become safe and secure from the very moment you give your heart to the Lord.

At this time, you will have been placed into the safety net of God, and nothing or anyone can remove you from that position. Not only this, but listen very carefully, when you accept the Lord into your heart and receive salvation, your name is written in the Lamb's Book of Life in heaven. It just doesn't get any better than that!

John 10:28-29 says,

> And I give unto them eternal life; and
> they shall never perish, neither shall any
> man pluck them out of my hand. My
> Father, which gave them me, is greater
> than all; and no man is able to pluck them
> out of my Father's hand.

Not only are you secure in Christ but also in God Himself. There is no greater security than this.

As this man continued to listen to the deacon, the struggle became more intense. The need for him to surrender his heart to the Lord was pressing upon him; however, the other stronghold was strongly pulling his heart in the other direction. For the third time, this man heard the words, "If you will just give Christ a chance." He pondered on those words once again and rehearsed in his life how he had tried different ways to cast away his problems. Then he reasoned within himself, I have tried everything and had not given Christ a chance to help me. He had come to the pinnacle point of decision in his life, when all of a sudden, he heard the voice of the Lord say to him, "This is your last chance." He had come to the crossroads of his life. If he refused this last calling of the Lord to salvation, it might be the last time he would ever hear or be inspired by the Lord for salvation.

The scriptures in the Bible tell us His Spirit will not always strive with man. I believe a man can refuse the calling of the Lord for the last and final time. An individual can cross the deadline with God, seal his fate, and preserve his destination to hell at the end of his life. I would like to backup what I am saying with an example. I have spoken with preachers aforehand who have told me about being called by friends or family members to a dying loved one's bedside. These preachers would do everything they could to persuade the dying soul to salvation. Those preachers would tell me they heard the dying one, tell them he could not be saved. He had turned away from the calling of the Lord and the wooing of the Holy Spirit in years gone by. Now the Lord was not present and could not be found.

This is why it is very important if one hears the calling of the Lord for salvation not to procrastinate and say to yourself, "I will come to the Lord when I have time or am ready." You might be taking a big chance the Lord will not be there for you when you decide to call upon Him. You might not know when it will be the last time you will hear the call of the Lord.

One must respond to the call of the Lord when He calls for you, not wait until you think you are ready or when you decide it is time, or that you'll decide to be saved when you're older. Proverbs 27:1 says,

> Boast not thyself of tomorrow: For thou knowest not what a day may bring forth.

One may think he has this much time or that much time to be saved. However, James 4:14 says,

> Whereas ye know not what shall be on the morrow. For what is your life? It is even a vapour, that appeareth for a little time, and then vanisheth away.

This verse is plainly telling us we don't know what tomorrow holds for us.

Job 14:1 says,

> Man that is born of a woman is of few days, and full of trouble.

We have no control of our next heartbeat or our next breath of air.

The Second Epistle to the Corinthians 6:2 says,

> For he saith, I have heard thee in a time accepted, and in the day of salvation have I succoured thee: behold, now is the accepted time; behold, now is the day of salvation.

This man tried to do things on his own, only to find nothing could satisfy. Hearing the man from the church saying for the third time, "If you will just give Christ a chance," hearing the Lord tell him it was his last chance, and remembering what little wisdom he possessed, he decided it might be best if he did give Christ a chance in his life.

He did not know how to pray, how to talk to God, or what to speak. He simply slipped out of the chair he was in and put himself into a prostrate position. With tear-filled eyes and humbleness of heart, he cried out to the Lord, asking Him to cleanse his heart, take him, and use him as He saw fit. That was his declaration of salvation.

He had just experienced the new birth or being reborn into the kingdom of God that the Bible speaks about. It is the only way a person can go to heaven. In Luke 15:10, Jesus said,

> Likewise, I say unto you, there is joy in the presence of the angels of God over one sinner that repenteth.

When a sinner repents and is reborn, their name is recorded in the Lamb's Book of Life. You are placed in the safety net of God, and one day, when your life is over on earth, you will spend an eternity in heaven with God, the Lord Jesus Christ, the Holy Spirit, and all your loved ones and friends who have gone on before you that have received salvation through Jesus Christ. When your name is added to the Lamb's Book of Life, nothing can ever change that. Your final destination is heaven.

After this man picked himself up, he sat down on the couch, looking at the man from church. He made this statement as he pointed his finger toward the little living room picture window, "I feel like going out there and telling everybody about Jesus Christ." He was a happy man.

This is one reason the Lord inspired him to write this book. It is an attempt to get the message of the salvation of the Lord to as many who would read his story and believe the message the Lord is sending to every heart. It is his desire that they might be introduced to the Lord, experience this new life in Christ, and have their names written down in the Lamb's Book of Life in order to sidestep hell and become heaven-bound.

You see, dear reader, he had come to the turning point in his life when he almost missed heaven. His ambition and hope in life is that you will not walk in his same shoes and almost miss heaven as well.

At this point of time in our story, I think it would be appropriate to introduce you to the man of our story. Dear friend and reader, the man of our story is none other than I, the author of this writing. I am a true witness of everything that has been penned down. I would like to briefly explain why man is in the position he is today.

God made man to be a special creation with whom He desired to have fellowship. After God had created the earth and set everything in order, He said in Genesis 1:26-28,

> And God said, Let us make man in
> our image, after our likeness: and let them
> have dominion over the fish of the sea,

and over the fowl of the air, and over the cattle, and over all the earth, and over every creeping thing that creepeth upon the earth. So God created man in his own image, in the image of God created he him; male and female created he them. And God blessed them, and God said unto them, Be fruitful, and multiply, and replenish the earth.

We continue in chapter 2.

And the Lord God formed man of the dust of the ground, and breathed into his nostrils the breath of life; and man became a living soul, And the Lord God planted a garden eastward in Eden; and there he put the man whom he had formed. And the Lord God said, It is not good that the man should be alone; I will make him an help meet for him. And out of the ground the Lord God formed every beast of the field, and every fowl of the air; and brought them unto Adam to see what he would call them: and whatsoever Adam called every living creature, that was the name thereof. And Adam gave names to all cattle, and to the fowl of the air, and to every beast of the field; but for Adam there was not found an help meet for him. And the Lord God caused a deep sleep to fall upon Adam, and he slept: and he took one of his ribs, and closed up the flesh instead thereof. And the rib, which the Lord God had taken from man, made he a woman, and brought her unto the man. (vss. 18-22)

As you recall, in the Garden of Eden, the Lord grew every tree that was pleasant to the sight and good for food, along with all the other herbs for food. However, there was one tree the Lord planted that was off limits to Adam and Eve—that was the tree of knowledge of good and evil. The Lord instructed them that if they would ever eat from this tree they would die.

The serpent, the old deceiver, tricked Eve into eating of this fruit, and then Eve got Adam to eat of the forbidden fruit of the tree. When God found out about this, He was distraught with them for disobeying Him. He put them out of the beautiful garden of plenty and cursed the ground, which made it hard for them to obtain their food.

Because of the choice they made, sin came upon all mankind. When we are born into this world, we inherit this sin nature. And once again, God leaves us with the choice to follow Him and live forever in the blissfulness of heaven, or reject His way and spend eternity in hell with all its torments.

Because of this sin nature, only the shedding of the blood and the sacrifice of Jesus is acceptable with God to cancel out our sin-debt. Jesus Christ has provided the way for us to be with Him in heaven one day. However, He has left the choice up to us—a simple yes or no on our part. Christ will not force you into a decision for Him but leaves that free-will choice for you.

I would like to take this time and share a few things with you that will insure your understanding how to make steadfast your way to heaven. First of all, I would like to establish one fact that the Bible makes very clear—there is only one way for you to go to heaven. We don't have to worry with doing this or doing that or contend with many different ways to confuse the way we have to go to get to heaven.

Jesus made that very clear and certain when He said in John 14:6,

> I am the way, the truth, and the life: no man cometh unto the Father, but by me.

We read in Isaiah 44:6,

> I am the first, and I am the last and beside me there is no God.

Also, in Acts 4:12 in the Bible says,

> Neither is there salvation in any other name under heaven given among men, whereby we must be saved.

The Bible also says that God is no respecter of persons, meaning there is no one individual accepted for salvation more than anyone else. It makes no difference who you are, what color your skin may be, or what nationality you are. God sees your heart.

In the Bible, Psalms 146:3-5 says,

> Put not your trust in princes, nor in the son of man, in whom there is no help. His breath goeth forth, he returneth to his earth; in that very day his thoughts perish. Happy is he that hath the God of Jacob for his help, whose hope is in the Lord his God.

Bringing this to our understanding means there is no hope whatsoever in mankind because the Bible says man was formed from dust of the earth, and when he dies, his body returns to the dust of the earth from which he came. So man has no power to help. His only help is to turn to the God of his creation by the way of the Lord Jesus Christ.

The highest level of man can only fail. There are many other scriptures throughout the Bible that explicitly state there is no other way into heaven except though the Lord Jesus Christ. In Proverbs 14:12, it states,

> There is a way which seemeth right unto a man; but the end thereof are the ways of death.

If a man thinks he can put his hope in a man or an organization or institution or a church or anything else, he will be eternally wrong and lose his own soul. One must even be careful of the various different and indifferent beliefs developed and introduced by man that can lead a man in the wrong direction. They can cause a man to deprive his soul from going to heaven.

One very important thing to remember is that man must make his choice for God in his lifetime. For once a man has expelled his last breath in this life, he will have sealed his destiny forever, and that will be the end of his hope for salvation.

One other thing of great importance to remember is this, it matters not what depth or level of sin you may find yourself in, how long you have lived in this condition of your sinful state, or how ungodly you think you might be. God can and will forgive you and save your soul if you will come to Him when He calls to you. You cannot entreat your salvation time as such one morning you get up, and you say to yourself, *I am going to get into my car and drive here or there.* Likewise, you get up one day, and you say to yourself, *I will get saved today.* It just doesn't work like that. When you experience the call of the Holy Spirit that becomes your accepted time for salvation. When the Holy Spirit of God calls to you, you will know it.

In the Bible, it says in 2 Corinthians 6:2,

> For he saith, I have heard thee in a time acccptcd, and in thc day of salvation have I succoured thee: behold, now is the accepted time; behold, now is the day of salvation.

John 6:44 states,

> No man can come to me, except the
> Father which hath sent me draw him: and
> I will raise him up at the last day.

You remember earlier in this writing that I was speaking of the man in this story who was experiencing a small, inner voice. This was the Holy Spirit drawing this man to God through Christ. This is why you must accept Christ when you notice the drawing—or conviction—in your soul. That is the Holy Spirit telling you it is the right time for salvation. You cannot just decide to be saved when you want to be saved. You may wait until it is too late.

Jesus said in John 3:18,

> And as Moses lifted up the serpent in
> the wilderness, even so must the Son of
> man be lifted up.

Then He said in John 12:32,

> And if I be lifted up from the earth I
> will draw all men unto me.

He was speaking of His crucifixion on the cross.

I truly believe everyone present on the earth, from the age of accountability onward, will, in their lifetime, experience the drawing of the Holy Spirit to Christ. Then it becomes your choice what you will do with Him.

And once again, I remind you, dear reader, that when you are aware the Lord is calling to you, that is the accepted time for your salvation. Hesitation and procrastination could cause you to lose your soul forever.

There are several scriptures in the Bible that will coincide with the verses found in Ephesians 2.

> For by grace are ye saved through faith; and that not of yourselves: it is the gift of God: Not of works, lest any man should boast. (vss. 8-9).

And so it is, as we have stated before, there is nothing we can do to earn our way into heaven. No, not one. Along with this is Acts 4:12.

> Neither is there salvation in any other: for there is none other name under heaven given among men, whereby we must be saved.

Titus 3:5 says,

> Not by works of righteousness which we have done, but according to his mercy he saved us, by the washing of regeneration, and renewing of the Holy Ghost.

One might also add 1 Timothy 2:5.

> For there is one God, and one mediator between God and men, the man Christ Jesus.

A mediator is a go-between from one person to another. Webster's Dictionary defines it as "to reconcile one to another." The only one qualified who could satisfy God and reconcile man to God is Jesus Christ.

Some may say within themselves that one cannot know if they are going to heaven or hell until they die. However, the verse found in 1 John 5 refutes this and says,

> These things have I written unto you that believe on the name of the Son of God; that ye may know that ye have eternal life, and that ye may believe on the name of the Son of God. (vs. 13)

This tells us that we can know on this side of the grave that we have eternal life in heaven that awaits our arrival after death.

In Mark 10, the disciples were asking Jesus who could be saved, and Jesus said to them in verse 27,

> With men it is impossible, but not with God: for with God all things are possible.

The Bible says the only way to heaven is through Jesus Christ. With all this being said, I would like to share with you some Scripture to help you find your way to be placed into the safety net of God, being heaven-bound.

I would like to say there is no sin ever thought of or practiced by any person God is not willing to forgive. There is a sin one can commit unto death; however, while you are still breathing God's air, you are given the opportunity to be forgiven and have a safety net placed around your soul forever. Only two things must be done for you to be placed into Gods safety net: you must believe that the God of all mankind sent His only begotten Son, Jesus Christ, to this earth to die by shedding His blood on the cross, and that He was buried and rose from the grave. So every sin you've ever committed can be forgiven and removed from your account.

Then you must ask the Lord Jesus Christ to forgive you for your sins and cleanse your heart. Thus, you experience the new birth, being the requirement to make heaven your eternal destination.

These two actions on your part will put you on the road to heaven.

With the blueprint of the Scriptures, it doesn't take long for one to understand that there may not be much more time left for earth dwellers before the Lord calls His children—all saved people who have called on Him for salvation—home to heaven.

Then those left behind will be here to experience and go through the twenty-one judgements outlined in the book of Revelation. These judgments will be hurled at all the earth and all earth dwellers. Believe you me, if you are left behind, you will wish over and over again, you would have heeded the call of the Lord in your lifetime by His Holy Spirit when you had the opportunity. The pain, the anguish, the tears, and the suffering that will be imposed on all who are left behind will not be like any catastrophic event that has ever touched the earth and earth dwellers.

I would like to leave you with a few verses from the Bible that will guide you to salvation in Jesus Christ.

> For God so loved the world, that he gave his only begotten Son, that whosoever believeth in him should not perish but have everlasting life. (John 3:16)

This simply means God loves people so much that after the fall of man caused sin to be dominant in the heart of every man, which put a separation between God and man and breached His relationship to them. He made a way for the relationship to be renewed.

Man will often try to become as perfect as he can on his own merits. Man's righteousness are not good enough or acceptable to God for him to be put back into a right relationship with God. Even the sacrifices of the blood of animals is not acceptable.

> For it is not possible that the blood of bulls and of goats should take away sins. (Heb. 10:4)

To try and put man back in the right relationship with God anything tainted with sin is not good enough. In fact, the Scriptures, Isaiah 64:6 states,

> But we are all as an unclean thing, and all our righteousnesses are as filthy rags.

So at the right time, God sent His only begotten Son, Jesus Christ, who knew no sin to shed His blood. This then is the only acceptable way for man to be placed back in good standing with God. So God Himself chose a virgin woman whose name was Mary for Jesus to be born to take on Himself a fleshly body as we have.

Remember the Christmas story when the Scriptures say in Luke 2:7,

> And she brought forth her firstborn son, and wrapped him in swaddling clothes, and laid him in a manger.

And the Scriptures speak about an angel of God who spoke to the shepherds who were watching over their sheep.

> I bring you good tidings of great joy, which shall be to all people. For unto you is born this day in the city of David a Saviour, which is Christ the Lord. (vss. 10-11)

At God's appointed time, Jesus was crucified on the cross, shedding His blood for the sin of the world—for your sins and mine.

In John 12:32, Jesus said,

> And I, if I be lifted up from the earth, will draw all men unto me.

Jesus was speaking of the day of His crucifixion on the earth. Jesus was crucified upon the cross between the two malefactors. The one man mocked the Lord and made fun of him. The other man realized the condition he was in that he was going to die for his wrong deeds and spend an eternity in hell. Luke 23:42-43 says,

> And he said unto Jesus, Lord, remember me when thou comest into thy kingdom. And Jesus said unto him, Verily I say unto thee, Today shalt thou be with me in paradise.

Believe in Jesus, repent of your sins, and one day when you die, you will be in the paradise of God. That is how simple it is to receive salvation from the Lord. Believe in Him, repent of your sins, and one day when you die, you will be in the paradise of God. The Bible goes on to explain in Romans 3:23 that

> All have sinned and come short of the glory of God.

This is telling us everyone is a sinner because we are born into sin, and no one is excluded—from the poorest peasant to the richest person living or who has ever lived. There is no difference between race or nationality. Everyone falls under this verse. Not one single person has ever measured up by man's way and become acceptable by God's standard. Not only do we not measure up to God's standard by falling short, but if we run our course in this life without any change, by not accepting Jesus as our Savior, we will receive wages for our sinful lives.

We all know that a wage is a form of payment for something we have earned or received in exchange for some service we have done. Wages are not always received in a monetary measure. Someone might give you a very nice expensive gift of some sort in exchange of some service done. Or they might give you the gift out of love, expecting nothing in return.

In the case of the verse in our discussion, it simply means that at the end of a person's sinful life, the wage received for this will be eternal death. Frankly, most people don't like to think of death. In most of us, it produces a type of fear because of the unknown and uncertainty of what comes after.

However, this type of death brings with it a separation of God forever with the punishment of being cast into an eternal hell and never being able to find any way out. My friend, you don't want to receive this type of wage.

This is what one can expect to receive by choosing man's way instead of God's way. We see the product of God's way in the second half of this verse—"the gift of God is eternal life through Jesus Christ our Lord."

This gift of God is something we don't have to work for. It is not a wage we can receive. It is a gift—a gift of eternal life, which is freely given to all who will accept God's only begotten Son, Jesus Christ, who died for our sins on the cross. Jesus removed the work out of our way to receive eternal life. As we already read in Ephesians 2:8-9,

> For by grace are ye saved through faith; and that not of yourselves: it is the gift of God: Not of works, lest any man should boast.

Remember the one malefactor on the cross who asked Jesus to remember him when he came into His kingdom? That malefactor received the free gift of salvation. He did not work for this free gift. He simply believed and asked the Lord. You can do the same thing and be set free from your burden of sin with heaven being your future.

The Scripture does not tell us about the second malefactor. We can only assume he did not entreat the Lord for his soul. So upon his death, his soul went to hell where he still is today.

This brings to mind what Jesus said to the malefactor that was on the cross beside Him, that he would be in paradise with Him today. There was no water baptism for that malefactor.

There are some folks who hold to the belief that being baptized by water plays a role in completing salvation. This would suggest to some that this constitutes a sort of work offered on their part to complete their salvation. However, Jesus provided the way of salvation for us without any form of help from us. The Bible states in Isaiah 64:6,

> But we are all as an unclean thing, and
> all our righteousnesses are as filthy rags.

There is nothing we can offer to aid in our salvation. Jesus Christ and His shed blood on the cross is all that is accepted by God as being sufficient to cleanse our sins.

The Scripture does not declare that we need to believe on the Lord Jesus Christ and be baptized in water to be saved. The Bible says we are to believe in Jesus, calling on Him only for salvation—plus nothing. A person who has accepted Jesus Christ as his savior and having been baptized by water afterward is merely confirming outwardly what happened inwardly.

One example of this is in the book of Acts, chapter 8, verses 26 through 38, where Philip is commissioned by an angel of the Lord to go to Gaza where he is to meet a man in a chariot from Ethiopia who is reading Scripture. We are told,

> Then Philip opened his mouth, and began at the same scripture, and preached unto him Jesus. And as they went on their way, they came unto a certain water: and the eunuch said, See, here is water; what doth hinder me to be baptized? And Philip said, If thou believest with all thine heart, thou mayest. And he answered and said, I believe that Jesus Christ is the Son of God. And he commanded the chariot to stand still: and they went down both into the water, both Philip and the eunuch; and he baptized him. (vss. 35-38)

I have said all this to explain that the malefactor who went to paradise with Jesus did so without being baptized with water. There are countless numbers of people who will be in heaven who have not been baptized by water.

A lot of people make this statement, "I believe in God," but do you know what the Bible says in James 2:19?

> Thou believest that there is one God; thou doest well: the devils also believe, and tremble. (James 2:19)

Believing that there is a God is well and good. You are halfway to salvation. John 1:10-12 says,

> He was in the world, and the world was made by him, and the world knew him not. He came unto his own, and his own received him not. But as many as received him, to them gave he power to become the sons of God, even to them that believe on his name.

So, my friend, the first step is to believe on Jesus. Second, you become complete in salvation when you receive Jesus as stated in Romans 10:9-10,

> That if thou shalt confess with thy mouth the Lord Jesus, and shalt believe in thine heart that God hath raised him from the dead, thou shalt be saved. For with the heart man believeth unto righteousness;

and with the mouth confession is made unto salvation.

We all know there will not be any devils in heaven. Also, there are verses that tell us of those who will also not be in heaven.

> Know ye not that the unrighteous shall not inherit the kingdom of God? Be not deceived: neither fornicators, nor idolaters, nor adulterers, nor effeminate, nor abusers of themselves with mankind, Nor thieves, nor covetous, nor drunkards nor revilers, nor extortioners, shall inherit the kingdom of God. (1 Cor. 9-10)

However, take notice of what verse 11 says,

> And such were some of you: but ye are washed, but ye are sanctified but ye are justified in the name of the Lord Jesus, and by the Spirit of our God.

As you have read the list of those who will not be in heaven, you might associate your life in one or all of them. This is what I am trying to convey to you. No matter what sin or sins you have found yourself participating in, you can and will be forgiven by doing what this verse says. If you will believe by faith that Jesus came here born of a virgin, died on the cross for your sins, and rose from the grave; you can ask Him to forgive you of your sins and save you. He will forgive you all your sins and save you that very moment and at the end of your life, you will go to Heaven.

There is no sin ever thought of or practiced by any person God is not willing to forgive. Jesus said in the book of John, chapter 14, verse 6,

> I am the way, the truth, and the life; no
> man cometh unto the Father, but by me.

This means you can do nothing at all on your own, attempt any other way to get to heaven, or add anything to what Jesus has already provided for you to go to heaven.

God has provided the way to heaven through Jesus Christ, but it is up to you to make that call and to make that choice. The Lord leaves the decision with you to make freely. Romans 10:13 says,

> For whosoever shall call upon the name
> of the Lord shall be saved.

In Titus 1:2, the Bible says,

> In hope of eternal life, which God, that
> cannot lie, promised before the world began.

There are many promises God has given us through His Word. He sent His only begotten Son, Jesus Christ, to earth to accept a fleshly body like ours. One day, He shed His blood on the cross of Calvary. All God asks of us is to believe on His Son, Jesus, in His death, burial, and resurrection, and He will grant us eternal life in heaven one day. Now, I ask you, how hard is that? The choice is yours alone. Are you willing to forfeit heaven for not doing something as simple as this?

Another important promise of God is in Philippians 1:6.

> Being confident of this very thing,
> that he which hath begun a good work in
> you will perform it until the day of Jesus
> Christ. (Phil. 1:6)

Once you have truly been saved, God will place in you His Holy Spirit to help you live a Christian life. Your name will be added to the Lamb's Book of Life in heaven, and nothing can ever take away your salvation.

A Word of Warning

He that rejecteth me, and receiveth not my words, hath one that judgeth him: the word that I have spoken, the same shall judge him in the last day. (John 12:48)

Don't be an unwise person and think you can live your life of sin, and just before you die, you can make your soul right with God. It doesn't always work like that. For one, you don't know when you will be called out of this body. You don't want to hear the words of the Lord saying to you, "Depart from me, go into everlasting punishment, for I never knew you."

Second, you have exhausted the time the Holy Spirit called to you for salvation. You crossed the deadline, and the Holy Spirit was not there when you wanted to be saved.

I encourage you, don't put off salvation another moment. Now you have the time to accept Jesus into your heart. If you drop into hell, you too will be begging like the rich man for a drop of water to cool your tongue because you are in torments in the flames of hell.

If you don't believe in hell, I promise you on the authority of God's Word that if you miss heaven, you will find out just how real hell is. Remember, only you can control the destiny of your soul by your choice.

> For it is written, As I live, saith the Lord, every knee shall bow to me, and every tongue shall confess to God. (Rom. 14:11)

If you do this now when you hear the Holy Spirit calling, you will be richer for it.

In closing, this day, while you are still breathing God's air, you are given another opportunity to be forgiven and have a safety net placed around your soul forever. If you find you need to ask Jesus to save you, you can do so right where you are. You must be sincere with Jesus at this moment. Simply ask Jesus to forgive you for all your sins, cleanse your heart, and make you ready for heaven.

After asking Jesus to save you, find a good Bible-preaching church, begin to read the Bible, and grow in the Lord. A good place to start reading in the Bible would be the book of John. Call upon the Lord while you still can, and sidestep hell. Don't miss out on heaven because you waited too long. I almost did—almost missing heaven!

Summary of Last Words

There has been approximately forty-nine years that have passed from the day of my salvation in Jesus Christ. If you recall, I mentioned in this writing that, first of all, I did not think or believe I could be saved. Second, I did not think I could stay saved.

The Lord is good to His Word and cannot and will not lie. He says in Hebrews 13:5,

> I will never leave you nor forsake you.

Also in Philippians 1:6, it says,

> Being confident of this very thing, that he [meaning Jesus] which hath begun a good work in you will perform it until the day of Jesus Christ.

And another promise Jesus made is in John 6:38-40,

For I came down from heaven, not to do mine own will, but the will of him that sent me. And this is the Father's will which hath sent me, that of all which he hath given me I should lose nothing, but should raise it up again at the last day. And this is the will of him that sent me, that every one which seeth the Son, and believeth on him, may have everlasting life: and I will raise him up at the last day.

Then in verse 47 Jesus continues,

Verily, verily, I say unto you, He that believeth on me hath everlasting life.

So, my friend, you can rest your weary heart and mind that when you are truly saved the Lord will send you the comforter—the Holy Spirit—to be with you the rest of your life. The Holy Spirit will help you, guide you, teach you the Word of God, and you will be blessed above measure. Give Christ a chance in your life, as I did, and you will experience the new birth, which Jesus spoke of in John 3:3.

> Verily, verily I say unto thee; except a man be born again he cannot see the kingdom of God.

Once you accept Christ as your saviour, your name will be written down in the Lamb's Book of Life. You will sidestep hell, and heaven will be your eternal home when your life here on earth has expired.

I'd like to share a poem I wrote for an activity with our Sunday school class.

To Capture a Dream

Once upon a time in years gone by
My hope and dream was to learn to fly.
With my love for the airplane, I entered the Air Force
Not knowing some pretty lassie would alter my course.
This lady I met while serving my time.
There was something about her that captured my mind.
Looking oft into her deep brown eyes,
She would sometimes take my mind away from the skies.
Each time I was with her, my heart grew fonder
Knowing someday I would have to leave
her for the wild blue yonder.
With my last assignment being across the sea,
I took the fond memory of her along with me.
In returning home from service to restart my life,
This lady I met, well, she became my wife.
One month into our marriage, I was turned again
Only to find Jesus, who became my Best Friend.
This woman who would do most anything I ask
With her whole heart she gave all to the task.
Through all these years, we have reaped God's blessings.
Sometimes, painful, while going through His testings.

This woman has stuck by me through thick and thin
And if I had to do it all over, I would marry her again.
This woman of whom I am speaking is Eunice by name.
She is as lovely as a flower sparkling in the rain.
After all those years have passed me by
Guess what! I still have a dream to capture the sky!

About the Author

Born in Dayton, Ohio, and raised on a farm in Greenville, Ohio, about thirty-five miles northwest of Dayton. He attended a Christian church as a young lad until the age of thirteen, when he decided there was no need to go to church any longer and just quit going. At the age of twenty-two, the Holy Spirit began to call to him, and by the age of twenty-four, he had lived for the devil for so many years and was so deep into sin he didn't think he could be saved. However, he did answer the call of the Lord and gave the Lord a chance in his life on July 14, 1970. God has proven to him that no matter how far down into sin one might find himself, He can and will forgive sins and save your soul, making an eternal home in heaven for you.

At the publishing of this book, Eunice and I have been married over 50 years. The Lord has blessed us with three children, Rachel, now living in Tennessee; Sarah, living in Florida and Timothy, living in Texas. We have a grandson, Peyton, in Tennessee and five grandchildren, Ethnan, Jacob, Brianna, Caleb and Nathaniel, in Florida.